The Colors of Water
The Shapes of Stone

poems by

Sandra Thaxter

Finishing Line Press
Georgetown, Kentucky

The Colors of Water
The Shapes of Stone

Copyright © 2018 by Sandra Thaxter
ISBN 978-1-63534-621-3 First Edition
All rights reserved under International and Pan-American Copyright Conventions. No part of this book may be reproduced in any manner whatsoever without written permission from the publisher, except in the case of brief quotations embodied in critical articles and reviews.

ACKNOWLEDGMENTS

The poems, 'Listening to Nora Jones', and 'No Expectations' were published by the Ibbetson Street press.

Publisher: Leah Maines
Editor: Christen Kincaid
Cover Art: Schulyer Thaxter
Author Photo: Willamain Somma
Cover Design: Elizabeth Maines McCleavy

Printed in the USA on acid-free paper.
Order online: www.finishinglinepress.com
also available on amazon.com

Author inquiries and mail orders:
Finishing Line Press
P. O. Box 1626
Georgetown, Kentucky 40324
U. S. A.

Table of Contents

Come 1

Islands 2

Photo by Willy Somma 3

Cheeserock 4

Listening to Nora Jones 5

Island Wedding 6

EE Cumming's Spring 8

Photo by Willy Somma 9

Summer Laundry 10

Mists in Time 11

Our Song from the North 13

Dreams in the House of My Father 15

Elegy to Sidney St. Felix Thaxter 16

Field of Grace 17

Photo by Schuyler Thaxter 18

Edna's Way 19

No Expectations 20

If Love 22

Garden 23

My Ashes 24

I am grateful to the women who came before me, those around me growing up, and now those I have come to know through living, poetry and my travels in Africa.

Come

and stay
at least until the tide
runs in and out.
Maybe stay longer
and watch the sunset
and the light on the white birches,
lithe dancers above the rocky shore,
where the tide runs in and out;
maybe watch
as the evening breeze
ruffles the sea and turns the leaves of trees.

Or go
before the next tide,
before we finish
our time
to watch
together.

When you are gone
remember
the dark water,
the angle of the sun,
the seaweed
rising and sinking
as the tide
comes in
and goes out
again.

Islands

Islands are spare places,
alone with the vast horizon,
hugging to their rock.

They stand to wind, and wind and waves,
and waves that keep coming
and retreating, and meeting again,
waves that comfort, waves that terrify,
waves that suck stones and debris
back into their foamy green.

The sea flings objects, debris
regurgitated and remade.
Islands hold things, tiny buds,
small creatures in tufts of grass,
and dwarf trees bent toward shelter.

Photo by Willy Somma

Cheese Rock

Our tender toes grasp the sharp spine,
as we climb the looming Cheese Rock,
ringed by its wet seaweed beard.
On top we stand seeking a spot
between the rust and black round holes.
We finger each sphere, and wonder
how they got here, on this one rock,
on this one island, in this place.

When the tide is high, we watch green
clear water swirl around and wash
in and out of crevices, rising up
over the outer rim, reaching
our toes, tossing seaweed about.

While we watch, sand castles and dams,
packed with rocks, melt away.
Our small feet seek a pathway
to descend the looming dark rust
pitted roof of our play place.

Listening to Nora Jones

In a place of rocks and wind,
a shelter warm with melodies.
Listening to Nora Jones.
A sweet explosion of tones
linger in the coffee grounds,
dissolving crusty boot tracked grit,
smoothing a day's end.
The sunlit isle three miles away,
is a rock. Halfway Rock sailors say.

Light of the fading day slips low into a trembling
evening glow, breezes ripple
the silver sea. Now see the shore
of Halfway Rock, a light,
a beacon on the edge of dark.

Soft piano octaves hover
beneath a simple melody.
A note is held, the sea is still.
Sound and light recolor the bay,
a long retard, breaks and reforms
in a rise of staccato strings.

White sail boats,
bright paper scraps.
tug on moorings.
Bows point east
on a ripple of mauve
and a flock of birds
flies into the wind.
A burst of orange,
the last of the sun -
Halfway Rock
is lit like fire.

Island Wedding

This spring morning
cool fog lingers
over hedges and lawns.
A wedding is in the air.
Bridal wreath white petals
drift down on damp grass.

The wedding day arrives.
The guests and bridesmaids
walk gingerly up the gravel path,
ladies carrying their shoes,
and men loosening their collars.
The youngest of the wedding,
just five, stiff in a pale organdy dress,
stands at the top of the stairs
with the wedding party.
She clutches her bouquet,
while the guests flow
in under the porches
around the sloping lawns
like seaweed in the tide.

Clouds gather, and rain
in great sheets rolls down
from the roof edge, trapping
the celebrants on the porch.
The wedding party
rushes into the living room
crushing together.
The noise and rustle suddenly stop.

The minister calls out to the bride and groom.
Now the vows are done,
the sun breaks out.
Doors are flung open.

The youngest of the wedding,
is jostled and tossed in the crowd,
a small flower in the bouquet of
taffeta, orchids and camellias,
ribbons and laughter.
Someone sings out: cut the cake!
"The cake, the cake where is it?"
She wonders.

Then they call for the rice.
It's time to throw the rice.
She asks, "What rice?
How do I throw the rice?"
She is running, running
down towards the boat
stumbling and crying
to throw the good luck
rice for the newlyweds.
The boat is leaving.
Rice is everywhere,
in the bride's hair,
on the groom's black tuxedo,
and in his pockets.

The bridesmaid opens
her small hands, still
grasping some grains of rice
and throws, as far as she can reach.

EE Cummings Spring

In Just —
        ust enough, maybe just enough of something fresh -
        the snowdrops give way to red tulips.
Spring
        the sun's shadow breathes in leftover winter -
Mud lucious —
        rain, fog threaten endless waiting
        while spring is poised.
Whistles far —
        where birds are
        chirping so brightly
and whee
        to tumble free.

Photo by Willy Somma

Summer Laundry

Why is it there
　hanging in the air?

A single sock
　　　at the end of the line?

I pass by it again, a sign
　　　suspended by a pin,
　　　still hanging there.

A thought left behind
　　　a forgotten note to a friend,
　　　the article I thought I'd send.

Mists in Time

Just here —
    perched on a stool,
    four square legs beneath,
    I sit precariously
    in the middle of morning.
    The past clings in whispers
    beneath my feet, rustling
    beyond my reach.
I sit still —
    in the mist of a past
    pasted into damp Maine mornings,
    a trembling child
    buttoned into thick wool
    and neck prickling collars.
    In a damp church yard
    she shivers in Sunday's gray chill,
    lost in a somber wash of adults
    in brown hats and dark coats,
    gathering up stray children.
    Relief comes in the back seat
    of a Studebaker, warm
    with squirming brothers
    anticipating sweet pancakes.
I dream —
    of my grandmother's house,
    finding my way through rooms
    where beds are mounded high
    with night blue silk puffs,
    where dressers rise up to the eaves,
    and books are neatly stacked.
    Gabled windows look out at the sky.

I hear —
    children rustling behind
    or under a bed. There are no voices,
    just the whispers and the scuttle of their feet.
I remember —
    a whiff of damp ruffled leaves
    on a day when the earth opened
    and let out its pungent breath.
    In a dark hallway closet, I inhale
    fresh winter in my father's overcoat.
I search —
    in bookcases, opening albums
    of leather, turning musty pages
    of old letters, and carefully folded
    crisp news clippings.
    From brown tinted photos of men,
    rigid behind dumbstruck daughters
    with great bows in their hair,
    women unsmiling, tightly coiffed,
    stare out at the unforeseeable.

A Song from the North

From Norway's bright hearths,
he blew in with Marie Louise,
a philosopher of harmonies
and lilting melodies,
gracious of manner.

We joined with his song,
we wove a bridal wreath
of rose petals spun
of our banter and laughter.

He came with his foreign tongue
and tall tales for children's ears,
He whistled and sang,
brightened days of rain,

His mop of curly hair
tossed in the air
A free spirit - he was
what we all wanted to be,
singing "Come Back Liza"
to his strawberry haired child
who rode on his shoulders,
her red rain boots
kicking as he strode.

He charmed us with Kierkegaard.
He stirred ideas
into wild live things,
slithering loose, breaking out
from the dusty walls of learning.

He sat with laborers protesting,
took to heart their cause.
He joined with wild youth singing
and beating their drums for change.

Now his Norwegian soul is part
of the glittering mountains,
where ice crystals fall in the spring
and rise again in the winter
as sparkling halos of light.

Dreams in the House of My Father

The house sits high on the brow of the land,
a full view of the harbor below.
Ships big and small ply their ways to the piers
on bright water and in evening's glow.

At the edge of the bay, trains rattle by,
boxcars with coal and logs piled high.
Wheels screech as they wind down through town.
Here stands the house of my father.

In my dreams I wander through doors,
in dark closets, opening secret drawers.
I hear echoes of voices, as I tumble through
a kaleidoscope of sounds and faces,
memories fresh with the smell of dark spaces.

There is a sun room lit by wide windows;
plants curl their leaves against the glass panes.
A photo stands on a white piano,
the bride and her groom hand in hand.

I lie on blue silken puffs under eaves
near books in soft leather of brown,
green, and rose stacked together.
The authors' name in gold letters bound:
Dana, Cooper, Scott, Hawthorne, Thoreau.

This is the town of Longfellow's poems:
where gentle streets go up and down,
Where a boy's will is wind's will
and all roads make their was to the sea.
The house sits high on the brow of the land
This is the house of my father.

Elegy to Sidney St. Felix Thaxter
b. Portland, Maine; 1883 - 1958

There's a view from the bank's top floor
onto clusters of tidy brick buildings,
built there in a century ago
along the once cobblestone streets,
leading to row after row of piers.
A fog hovers over the slate roofs,
wet and nestled against each other.

I entered this top floor entry hall
held breathless by your portrait
filling the tall paneled wall
in this law office, where your son,
and grandson have practiced.

Your eyes look straight ahead
from the portrait's elegant frame.
From those expressive eyebrows
a look asks me to stop and listen now.

But you are the listener,
with passion for the law,
considering human lives in balance,
with logic and eloquent language,
and deep compassion for human flaws.

The black robes are thick,
pleats fall to your feet.
The draped sleeves
cover your hands.
The robes weigh heavy,
as in full posture you stand.
Your presence rises to meet
my questions and day's damp fog
that clings.

Field of Grace

Tall stately stems
making way, one
for the other, for the other,
bending and twisting around another.
Daisies yearning through lacy spray
where yellow snapdragons hover
just below the Queen's Lace
and red tipped hay,
shy amidst the sturdy stocks.
Each seeking a place
knowing not the larger scheme,
seeing not the grace
of willing bending,
of texture and hue:
burnt ocher, cream with green,
all rolling together with the afternoon,
the only gardener, water, wind and sky.

Photo by Schuyler Thaxter

Edna's Way
> *(Edna St. Vincent Millay)*

Edna's way was fierce as winter.
inhaled on the rocky coast of Maine.
To live there is to go outside and see,
to face of winds and the steely sea,
the dark beneath three hills rising

Edna, the oldest of three young girls,
their mother away in the cold night.
The tales Edna must have heard,
she must have known of the cries and pain,
from islanders sick far from help. The wind blew
cold beneath the door. Shawls held close,
feet stretched to embered stoves, three sisters
made warmth from shared breath.

No Expectations

I packed a few things,
a book of new poems
tucked away with my sandals
and shirt for our day.
What to expect?
Imagined possibilities rise
from long abandoned hopes
like bubbles in Perrier.

No expectations
you said.

I'll take the boat
across the bay —
will you be waiting
when I come in?

It's been ten years
since we parted.
You were going to Africa.

The gouda cheese I bought —
will it be enough for lunch?
Or will we have a glass of wine?
Just walk around,
you said.

I don't know what you'll think
of my hair gone frizzy gray.
So much I could say, but here I am.
The boat fare six dollars.

It's too much
for such a short way.
I should swim
the entire mile,
emerge like a seal,
sleek — and smile
at your surprise.

Did you remember
that today I would come?
Will you still be so tall and thin,
waiting at the top of the gangway?

It's only me,
with my faded Bosox hat
and crinkly toes.
How long is it
since we dug in the low tide slime
and listened to the seashells hum?

And you
dripped castles of mud,
threw sand in my hair;
your laughter sparkled
while the sea wiped bare
our greatest designs.

Will you smile and wave
when the boat comes in
and the captain throws the line.
I'll be the first off the boat,
if I can — No expectations.

If Love

if love
  can be pressed into eggplant parmigiana
  or tenderly simmered with fagioli.

if happiness
  is the opening of an aluminum door
  or reeling in salt-sweetened towels on a summer afternoon,

if life is the harnessing of hearts
  where peaches ripen on the window sill
  and fading photos are gently tacked up again
  and softly spoken wisdoms pile up,

then
  we have been given life and love.

Garden

It's overgrown that garden you love so.
See lilies lost and limp beneath weigela,
the clematis run round and up and down,
the privet rise waving to the clouds.

How does the hand restore the grace,
the sweet intimacy of tender blooms?.
The knife, the choppers,
the shaping scissors wait.
It's overgrown that garden you love so.

My Ashes

will not be contained
by some bronze urn.
No, they will be gathered
like a gray flock
poised on the cusp of the sea.
They will rest in an open bowl
on a stone etched with my name,
face to the southwest winds,
back to the northeast.
They will go where the wind goes.

The stone
will be warmed by the sun,
and surrounded by sweet grass
holding tight their bursting seeds.
The moon
will shine brightly on its face,
the lapping waves
murmuring their parting songs.

I do not fear this place.
This is no official burial ground
It is where my ashes will fly free.
No one will define the plot,
choose the boundaries,
just the wind
just the day.

Some child,
who doesn't know my name,
will stand on this windy bluff —
raise her arms
and sing to the wind.

Sandra Thaxter lives in Newburyport, Massachusetts. She was born in Portland, Maine, and continues to spend summers on an island in Maine.

She has been writing for many years, but this is her first published collection. She studied poetry and writing in New York City at the Poetry Project at St. Marks, and at the 92nd street Y. She also attended the Great Heron Writing Workshop in Antigonish, Nova Scotia, with writers from Newfoundland and Cape Breton.

Currently she is studying with Alfred Nicol, and Rhina Espaillat of the Powow Poets. She has attended the Frost Farm spring poetry weekend in New Hampshire. Her academic background was in languages and comparative literature, as well as software engineering. In addition to poetry, she is engaged in social justice work and a non-profit supporting education projects in Africa.

The poems, 'Listening to Nora Jones', and 'No Expectations' were published by the Ibbetson Street press.

"I write as an attempt to tell truths and uncover the struggle and joy that makes us human. I believe that we are formed by the places where we live and learn about ourselves in nature's harsh edges and delicate beauty. I also experience poetry as a form of peacemaking, as poetry helps us process the chaos and injustice that is part of our own making."

www.ingramcontent.com/pod-product-compliance
Lightning Source LLC
LaVergne TN
LVHW041520070426
835507LV00012B/1708